A Gift for

Helen Bliss

From

Rose Minion

Date

Oct 26, 2000

Happy Birthday

Visit Tyndale's exciting Web site at www.tyndale.com

Whisper a Prayer for Friends

Copyright © 2004 by Mark Gilroy Communications, Inc.

Photography credits:
Pages: Cover, title page, 10, 84, 90 © by Alamy; Pages 4, 12, 16, 22, 26, 32, 38, 44, 46, 48, 50, 54, 56, 58, 68-69, 76, 78, 80, 86 © by Photos.com; Pages: 8, 28, 40-41, 52, 66, 74, 92 © by Digital Vision; Pages: 14, 20, 30, 34, 36, 42, 62, 64, 82, 88-89 © by Image State; Pages: 24, 68, 70, 72 © by Michael Hudson; Pages: 60, 94 © by Photodisc. All rights reserved.

Designed by Beth Sparkman

ISBN 0-8423-8296-8

Printed in Italy

09 08 07 06 05 04
6 5 4 3 2 1

no greater love

Whisper a Prayer
FOR FRIENDS

 TYNDALE HOUSE PUBLISHERS, INC.
WHEATON, ILLINOIS

I myself have gained much joy and comfort from your love.

Philemon 1:7, NLT

Introduction:
I Thank God for You

We've been friends through the ups and downs of life.
We've laughed and cried together. It's been great,
hasn't it?

When I think about you, I can't help but smile
and thank God for our friendship.

The following prayers communicate just a little
of what I've already said to God on your behalf. I
hope they help you feel loved and protected, and
help you express your own cares, joys, and thanksgiving to God.

God's peace is wonderful beyond understanding.
To experience it, all we have to do is whisper a
prayer.

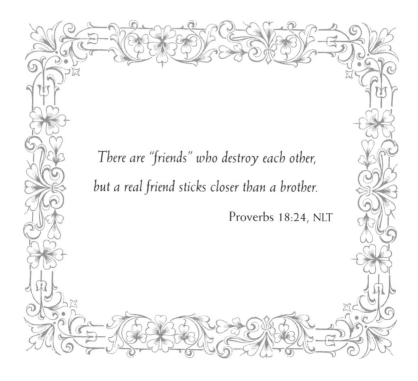

There are "friends" who destroy each other,

but a real friend sticks closer than a brother.

Proverbs 18:24, NLT

My Friend

Dear God,

My prayer today is that you would help my friend . . .

- ◆ forgive those who have wronged her,
- ◆ receive the comfort she needs for any of life's hurts,
- ◆ receive from me and other friends the spiritual support and encouragement for the challenges she will face,
- ◆ sense my gratitude because she has taught me so much about your goodness and love.

And, God, please help me to return that love to her and to others.

Look at the birds of the air, for they neither sow nor reap nor gather into barns; yet your heavenly Father feeds them. Are you not of more value than they?

Matthew 6:26, NKJV

He Watches Over You

Dear Heavenly Father,

Thank you for watching over us. We are not without food, clothing, or shelter because you meet every one of our needs.

I pray today that my friend will realize just how valuable she is to you. I pray that she will be aware of just how much you care for her. I pray that she will grow in her faith in you as a good and kind God.

When we are tempted to worry about the various needs of our lives, may we remember that you care for the birds of the air—and you love us even more!

Two are better than one,

Because they have a good reward for their labor.

For if they fall, one will lift up his companion.

But woe to him who is alone when he falls.

Ecclesiastes 4:9-10, NKJV

Never Alone

Dear Heavenly Father,

You alone can be counted on to be there for us in every moment and situation of life. As humans, we aren't always aware of the needs in others' lives— or if we are, we don't always know how to help.

And yet we really do need each other. You have created us to support one other, to help each other with burdens and hurts. Our concern, our kindness, our presence truly make a difference.

I pray that I will always be a person my friend can turn to for support. Help her to see your love through my life.

Consequently, you are no longer foreigners
and aliens, but fellow citizens with God's
people and members of God's household.

Ephesians 2:19, NIV

God's Household

Father God,

I thank you right now for my incredible friend
who . . .

- ◆ comforted me when I was hurting,
- ◆ provided support when I was weak,
- ◆ confronted me when I was spiritually drifting,
- ◆ gave me confidence when I didn't believe in myself,
- ◆ offered me friendship when I was lonely,
- ◆ showed me truth when I was confused,
- ◆ prayed with me when I faced problems,
- ◆ counseled me when I needed direction.

When I see my friend, I am reminded of what a privilege it is to be a member of your awesome household.

The steps of the godly are directed by the Lord.

He delights in every detail of their lives.

Though they stumble, they will not fall,

for the Lord holds them by the hand.

Psalm 37:23-24, NLT

You Will Not Fall

Dear Lord,

Thank you for directing our steps; for helping us navigate the difficult paths of life; for allowing us to stand, even when circumstances would knock us down; for holding us by the hand through your love and kindness.

When my friend stumbles, help her not to fall. I ask that she would sense your closeness and your love even in the tough times.

We will walk with confidence, knowing that you are at work even in the smallest details of our lives.

Are you tired? Worn out? Burned out on
religion? Come to me. Get away with me and
you'll recover your life. I'll show you how to
take a real rest. Walk with me and work with
me—watch how I do it.

Matthew 11:28-29, *THE MESSAGE*

16

Rest for the Soul

O Lord,

You know that we sometimes become burdened with a sense of weariness. We're not sure how we can get everything done. We don't feel like we have anything left to offer.

Thank you for inviting us to bring our burdens to you. Thank you for having the empathy to know that when we get tired we sometimes struggle to express our faith and hope. Yet you still accept and embrace us as we are, and you offer to carry our loads with us.

O Lord, I pray that you will bless my friend with rest for her body and soul.

Do not forget to do good and to share with

others, for with such sacrifices God is pleased.

Hebrews 13:16, NIV

Pleasing God

Merciful God,

You are an awesome God, full of compassion and
kindness. Your love and mercy know no bounds. Your
heart is always turned toward those who are hurting
and those who have serious needs.

We want to do good deeds and reach out to
others, but sometimes we get so caught up in our own
lives that we forget to act.

I ask that you renew in my heart—and in my
friend's heart—a loving sense of compassion. Give us
the strength to do something about it.

As we share with the needy, we will also remember to praise you for the many blessings you have
given us.

Be strong and courageous. Do not be afraid or terrified because of them, for the Lord your God goes with you; he will never leave you nor forsake you.

Deuteronomy 31:6, NIV

Courage

O Lord Our God,

With you on our side, we have absolutely nothing to fear, though at times we do take our eyes off you and begin to lose heart.

You know the neglected areas of our lives where we need to stretch and grow. You know the challenges we need to own up to and face. You know the uncertainties about the future that we feel.

Would you give courage to my friend so that she knows without a doubt in her heart that you do go ahead of her and lead the way? Thank you for guiding and protecting her.

The Lord is my shepherd, I shall not be in want.

He makes me lie down in green pastures,

he leads me beside quiet waters, he restores my soul.

Psalm 23:1-2, NIV

Green Pastures

Gentle Shepherd,

How wonderful it is to stop each day to spend time alone with you in prayer and in your Word. You are such a good shepherd, who knows when we need rest, when we need to pull away from the noises of life to experience peace and quiet.

Please remind us when we need to turn off the radio or television or stop looking at a computer screen. Remind us that the deepest need of our lives is not any material possession we don't have, but to draw close to you—for then everything else takes care of itself.

Thank you for gently leading my friend to green pastures and quiet waters today.

How great is the love the Father has lavished

on us, that we should be called children of God!

1 John 3:1, NIV

Your Child

Abba Father,

I am amazed by the love you have for us. Just as a mother cherishes her child in her heart, you cherish us in your heart.

You feel the same love—but so much more—for us. It is humbling and an honor that you call us your children, that you truly are a Daddy to us.

Today, please bring joy and happiness to my friend as she realizes again what a wonderful, loving Father you are to her.

As iron sharpens iron, a friend

sharpens a friend.

Proverbs 27:17, NLT

Sharp As Iron

Dear God,

The very best relationships are the ones where friends help each other grow.

Thank you for my friend, who really does help me become the person you have created me to be. I pray that we will build each other up in our relationships, our wisdom, our emotional maturity, our skills, our poise, our service, our compassion, and most of all, in our love for you.

Make us gentle as doves—but sharp as iron!

A friend loves at all times.

Proverbs 17:17, NKJV

Always Loved

Dear God,

You showed us what true love is when you sent your Son, Jesus Christ, to die for our sins. I pray that I will reflect that same kind of love for my friend . . .

- ◆ even if we disagree,
- ◆ even if it is not convenient,
- ◆ even when I'm tempted to focus on only my own needs,
- ◆ even if she is struggling to receive love at a particular moment.

God, it is wonderful to have a friend—and even more so, a God—who loves at all times!

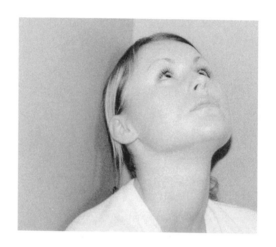

There is therefore now no condemnation to those who are in Christ Jesus, who do not walk according to the flesh, but according to the Spirit.

Romans 8:1, NKJV

Not Guilty

Dear God,

When we were lost and without you, you called out to each one of us with words of mercy, forgiveness, and healing. May we never forget the moment that we truly recognized how empty life is without you.

God, it is so easy to live in the flesh, relying solely on our own thoughts, our own wants, our own strength. But when the Holy Spirit dwells in our hearts, a whole new world opens before us. We discover a dimension of life—our spiritual nature—which we only suspected before.

God, I know that there are times when my friend's own thoughts and feelings of inadequacy—or the words of others—will make her feel condemned. Please remind her that in her heart and spirit she is united with Jesus Christ, and that he offers her life and forgiveness, not death and guilt.

But as for me, it is good to be near God.

Psalm 73:28, NIV

Near to God

My God,

I pray that my friend will not build her self-esteem on the basis of material possessions or personal accomplishments—or even on the blessings of cherished friends and family members.

Help her to affirm that knowing you is her ultimate source of hope, joy, love, faith, confidence, success, and every other blessing. With you in our hearts, our lives need never be the same.

No matter what tough challenges my friend faces—or how great the joys she experiences—draw her near to you, O God.

Peace I leave with you; My peace I give to

you; not as the world gives, do I give to you.

John 14:27, NASB

Divine Peace

Dear God of All Peace,

The world is in turmoil—and there are areas of our lives that don't feel very peaceful right now. Too often we look elsewhere to try to achieve peace—entertainment, family and friends, our own discipline and inner resources.

Yet you sent your Son, Jesus, as the one way to peace in our world—and in our lives. He alone provides a contentment that is not dependent on what is happening around us.

Thank you so much for helping my friend put her focus back on Jesus and receiving the peace that always follows. Dear God, your gifts truly are the best.

love

compassion

God so loved the world that he gave his only
Son, so that everyone who believes in him will
not perish but have eternal life. God did not
send his Son into the world to condemn it,
but to save it.

John 3:16-17, NLT

Loving Our World

Dear God,

I know that there are so many things happening in the world today that break your heart or anger you.

When we see reports of violence, cruelty, exploitation, and negligence, we are saddened and angered—but remind us not to become judgmental. We do not excuse or ignore evil, but if your purpose in sending your Son was not to condemn the world, then condemnation should not be our purpose either.

I ask that you help my friend and me to be redemptive—to see the world through your eyes of love and compassion. When we begin to condemn others, help us to pray for their salvation instead.

Those who become Christians become new persons. They are not the same anymore, for the old life is gone. A new life has begun!

2 Corinthians 5:17, NLT

A New Life

Dear Father,

How amazing that you not only come into our lives to save us from our sins, but you also make us into new persons. I pray that my friend will . . .

- ◆ discover the various ways you have made her a beautiful new person,
- ◆ let go of anything from her old life that is harmful,
- ◆ experience the joy and confidence that come from knowing you are at work in her life.

We praise you and thank you today for the blessing of receiving new life in Christ Jesus!

Those who wait on the Lord
shall renew their strength;
they shall mount up with wings like eagles,
they shall run and not be weary,
they shall walk and not faint.

Isaiah 40:31, NKJV

40

Soaring

O Mighty Lord,

Would you give to us a renewed strength, vision, optimism, joyfulness, determination, courage, sense of humor, confidence, love, kindness, compassion, playfulness, faith, friendliness, gentleness, patience, and all the other dynamics that make us a light in the world?

Even though we come to you feeling weary, just talking to you, spending time with you, waiting before you give us a sense of hope.

Lord, remind my special friend today that she can do so much more than just get by—with your strength, she can soar!

He is their shield, protecting those who walk
with integrity. He guards the paths of justice
and protects those who are faithful to him.

Proverbs 2:7-8, NLT

Protect Us

Dear Lord,

There is an evil one in our world who is committed to destroying our lives. So many have fallen under Satan's influence and do his dirty work for him.

You are a mighty shield. And you are more powerful than any force of evil. When we walk in your ways, when we turn to you with our trust and faith, you are always there to help us.

Lord, I pray a special protection for my friend today. Guard her paths. Protect her from all forms of harm, whether it be physical danger or spiritual temptation. Thank you for being her shield.

I can do all things through Christ

who strengthens me.

Philippians 4:13, NKJV

Feeling Inadequate

Mighty God,

You have promised not to allow challenges, burdens, or temptations to come our way without also providing us the strength to handle them.

But many times we lack the strength to triumph over our circumstances—when we've not exhibited the poise and grace that should characterize a believer. Then we look at people around us who seem to have it all together, and our feelings of inadequacy increase.

It's so amazing that when we recognize our lack of personal power and confess our need of you, you step in to do for us what we cannot do ourselves.

Dear God, I pray that my friend will turn to you as her source of strength. Grant her the faith and confidence to declare that she can do all things because you make her more than adequate for her tasks.

Shout with joy to the Lord, O earth!

Worship the Lord with gladness.

Come before him, singing with joy.

Acknowledge that the Lord is God!

He made us, and we are his.

We are his people, the sheep of his pasture.

Psalm 100:1-3, NLT

Shout to the Lord

O Lord God,

You are great and wonderful. You deserve all our worship and praise. When we come before you with adoration and gratitude, we become new people—better people. Even as we give to you what is yours to receive, you give us back so much more in return.

Today we acknowledge that you are our creator—and we belong to you. We will worship you with enthusiasm, gladness, thanksgiving, and singing throughout the entire day.

I pray that my friend will experience a renewed sense of peace and purpose as she shouts with joy to you.

If you, God, kept records on wrongdoings,

who would stand a chance? As it turns out,

forgiveness is your habit, and that's why

you're worshiped.

Psalm 130:3-4, *THE MESSAGE*

Your Forgiveness

Dear God,

I am so amazed at the depth of your love for us. You are so extravagant in your kindness toward us that you choose to forget our sins. Once you forgive us, you no longer keep a record of our wrongdoings. Thank you so much for being a God of second chances.

Help me not to harbor sin in my life out of fear and embarrassment. Remind me that you wait for me, with arms open wide, to simply ask you to forgive my wrongs.

Help my friend to receive from you today everything that she needs in her life—including your gracious gift of forgiveness.

I will make you a great nation;

I will bless you

And make your name great;

And you shall be a blessing.

Genesis 12:2, NKJV

You Are a Blessing

O Lord,

You promised our spiritual father, Abraham, that you would bless him in order that he would be a blessing to others.

Would you bless my friend today? Would you help her feel your presence? Would you give her a renewed sense of joy? Would you meet any physical, emotional, or spiritual needs that she has right now? And would you help her have a profound sense of your purpose for her life?

O Lord, my friend is a blessing to me and to others. Thank you for making our lives so rich and meaningful.

O Lord, you are so good, so ready to forgive,

so full of unfailing love for all who ask your aid.

Psalm 86:5, NLT

Unfailing Love

Dear Lord,

So many times we don't receive what we most need from you because we fail to ask for your help. But you invite us to come boldly before you, bringing every care and concern that we have.

You are a good God. You are always ready to forgive and save.

Today, I ask you to help my friend with any relationship problems, with any challenges or situations that require your intervention, with any personal failings or sin. And grant her the grace and strength to forgive others just as you have forgiven her.

An anxious heart

weighs a man down,

but a kind word

cheers him up.

Proverbs 12:25, NIV

A Kind Word

O Lord,

How easy it is to let the troubles of this world dominate us. We lose the joy of our salvation and our spirit becomes heavy. We hold tightly to anxieties and fears that you don't intend to be part of our lives.

I pray that my friend would have the faith and confidence to lay before you any issues that have created an anxious heart in her—and to have the trust and calm assurance that you have everything, including her life, under control.

And, Lord, give me that kind word that will ease her anxiety and bring a smile to her face.

I love the Lord because he hears

and answers my prayers.

Because he bends down and listens,

I will pray as long as I have breath!

Psalm 116:1-2, NLT

He Hears You

Gracious Lord,

May my friend know the grace, comfort, and joy that come by simply talking to you in prayer each day. May her prayer life become so real to her that it's not merely a block of time or a duty but an ongoing conversation with you throughout her day.

I pray that neither of us will go back to living solely off our own resources, not remembering that you are always present to hear and answer our prayers. You have bent down near to us and allowed us to glimpse your presence in our lives. Thank you!

Let my friend know that you hear her as she expresses her worship, her gratitude, and her needs to you.

Celebrate! Worship and recommit to God!

Nahum 1:15, *THE MESSAGE*

joy

laughter

Celebrate!

Heavenly Father,

You have not created and redeemed us to live dull, gray, joyless, plodding lives. Oh yes, we know you want us to be true to our vows, but you don't want us to take life or ourselves so seriously that joy and laughter are squeezed from our souls.

Thank you for creating a world filled with wonder and delight. Thank you for family and friends that make our lives so rich. Thank you that you want us to find pleasure in following your will and ways.

And thank you that you have invited my friend to join the celebration of life you have created for our enjoyment.

Don't worry about anything; instead, pray about everything. Tell God what you need, and thank him for all he has done. If you do this, you will experience God's peace, which is far more wonderful than the human mind can understand.

Philippians 4:6-7, NLT

No Worries

Dear God,

When you remind us not to worry, we are tempted to laugh, because worry comes so easily to us! Forgive our lack of faith.

You invite us to pray about everything, to tell you exactly what we need, to thank you for all you have done for us already and for all you are going to do in the days ahead.

I pray that today my friend will set aside her worries—about her family, about her finances, about needs among her friends—and I thank you right now that you offer her your peace, which is far more wonderful than our minds can understand.

We pray this in order that you may live a life
worthy of the Lord and may please him in
every way: bearing fruit in every good work,
growing in the knowledge of God.

Colossians 1:10, NIV

Walking Worthy

Lord,

You have been so kind and gracious toward us that we want to please you, to walk worthy of you, in every area of our lives.

I ask that you would help my friend and me . . .

- ◆ exhibit integrity in all our dealings,

- ◆ treat others with respect and kindness,

- ◆ share your love and forgiveness with the lost of the world,

- ◆ be effective in every area of life, but especially in our service to you,

- ◆ grow in our knowledge of who you really are.

Unless the Lord builds a house,

the work of the builders is useless.

Unless the Lord protects a city,

guarding it with sentries will do no good.

Psalm 127:1, NLT

Lord, We Need You

Dear Lord,

We do our best to build solid homes and families. We use the wisdom and common sense you have given us to protect ourselves, improve ourselves, and advance ourselves.

But we understand and affirm that ultimately, even after we have done our best, you alone provide the security, creativity, healing, salvation, protection, inspiration, self-worth, and guidance that we need to build a great life.

Today I again acknowledge my desperate need of you. Build my life as you would have me to live it. And I bring my friend before you, asking that you bless and protect her this day.

We can make our plans, but the Lord

determines our steps.

Proverbs 16:9, NLT

Our Plans

O Lord,

You give us intelligence and expect us to use our brains to make the best decisions for our lives. You give us the wisdom and energy to plan ahead.

But it is awe-inspiring to know that after we've done the very best we can, you truly guard and guide our steps. There are times when things don't turn out the way we planned, but through you, they turn out even better. We make our plans, but you direct our steps.

I pray that my friend will keep doing the best she can—and trust you with all her heart.

If my people who are called by my name will humble themselves and pray and seek my face and turn from their wicked ways, I will hear from heaven and will forgive their sins and heal their land.

2 Chronicles 7:14, NLT

Heal Our Land

Dear God in Heaven,

You know the condition of our world. You know the state of our nation. We are so blessed, so prosperous, and so advanced. But you also know the dark side of our land: Infidelity, broken families, greed, corruption, abuse, and so many forms of immorality dominate our cultural landscape.

Teach us to be humble and pray. Help us to turn from any ways that are not pleasing to you.

We pray that you would forgive and heal our nation—and that you would begin that work in us.

He was wounded for our transgressions,

He was bruised for our iniquities;

the chastisement for our peace was upon Him,

and by His stripes we are healed.

Isaiah 53:5, NKJV

By His Stripes

Lord,

How easy it is for us to blame others for the problems of the world. How tempting it is to proclaim our innocence and refuse to accept responsibility for our actions.

You gently remind us that everyone has sinned and gone astray—our lives have not been blameless. Everyone is deserving of punishment.

And yet you gave your Son to pay the price for our transgressions. O Lord, I pray that my friend would thank you all the days of her life as she receives the salvation, the peace, the restoration, and the healing that are hers through the suffering and blood of Jesus.

Through the Lord's mercies we are not consumed,

because His compassions fail not. They are

new every morning; great is Your faithfulness.

Lamentations 3:22-23, NKJV

New Each Day

Merciful Lord,

You promise to give us new mercies every single morning of our lives. We don't have to store up grace, mercy, or faith from yesterday. Your fresh touch upon us is up-to-date every day.

We receive your mercies today with a deep sense of gratitude and appreciation—knowing full well how much we need them. And whether our days are tough or easy, we don't ever want to take this gift from you lightly or for granted.

May my friend rejoice and give you praise, O Lord, for the tender mercies that are hers just for knowing and trusting you.

A gentle answer turns away wrath, but harsh words stir up anger. . . . Gentle words bring life and health.

Proverbs 15:1, 4, NLT

Gentle Words

Dear God,

When I think of times I have not controlled my tongue, when I have lashed out in anger at my family or friends, I am truly embarrassed and sorry. I know that harsh words only stir up more anger. Please forgive me.

I pray that my friend will speak words that bring life and health to her husband, to her children, to her friends—even to casual acquaintances. May her speech be wise and filled with grace.

Through your words my life has been changed forever. I pray that, in some small way, my words will bless the friend I love so much.

Watch out! Be very careful never to forget what you have seen the Lord do for you. Do not let these things escape from your mind as long as you live! And be sure to pass them on to your children and grandchildren.

Deuteronomy 4:9, NLT

Don't Ever Forget

Dear Lord,

Oh, how easy it is to forget what you have done in our lives. When we face challenges, we are tempted to be fearful and complain about our lot in life. When everything is going great, we are tempted to take all the credit and not acknowledge our need of you.

Give us a spirit of remembering. Help us to remember your mighty deeds throughout history. You are truly a God of miracles and redemption.

Help us to always remember what you have done in our lives—and to share our stories with others that they would open their hearts to you.

A cheerful heart is good medicine.

Proverbs 17:22, NLT

Laughter

Wise God,

Thank you for creating laughter to brighten our lives. There are times for being somber, respectful, and appropriately serious, but you also invite us to cut loose, to celebrate, smile, and laugh at the humor and levity of life.

Today we acknowledge that you are God—and you have the world under control. We're not going to worry, judge, or walk around with a scowling face. We're going to laugh at jokes—and even tell a few of our own—because you made us to be cheerful.

Dear God, would you bring a refreshing and healing touch to my friend through your gift of laughter.

Be kind and compassionate to one another,

forgiving each other, just as in Christ God

forgave you.

Ephesians 4:32, NIV

Tenderhearted

Dear God,

How easy it is to take to heart the slights and offenses we receive from others and become defensive, closed, and cynical. We all have been hurt and bear emotional scars to prove it.

You have not created us to hold grudges and allow anger to fester in our lives. Because of what you have done for us through Jesus Christ, we are able to move beyond feelings of resentment and vengeance to forgiveness of others. When we are tempted to hold tightly to our hurts, remind us of what Jesus did for us on the cross.

May my friend experience the peace that comes from receiving your forgiveness and passing that forgiveness on to others.

Let us not grow weary while doing good, for

in due season we shall reap if we do not lose heart.

Galatians 6:9, NKJV

Don't Give Up!

Dear Lord,

I pray that my friend won't ever give up . . .

- ◆ even if her friends forsake her,
- ◆ even if she struggles with a loved one for a season,
- ◆ even if her church experiences problems and strife,
- ◆ even if her life doesn't measure up to what you expect from her and what she expects from herself.

You have planted seeds of faith and grace through her life, and you have promised that if she persists, there will be a successful harvest in the right season.

Weeping may endure for a night,

But joy comes in the morning.

Psalm 30:5, NKJV

Joy Comes in the Morning

God of Comfort,

When our hearts are filled with sorrow, it's so easy to let discouragement dominate our spirits.

We sometimes forget that you are at work on our behalf, even in our toughest and most painful moments. Most importantly, you are at work in our lives, making us into the persons you want us to become.

This morning is a wonderful reminder that you are a God of healing and renewal. Thank you so much for giving my friend and me a new sense of joy and a new perspective on life.

If God cares so wonderfully for flowers that are here today and gone tomorrow, won't he more surely care for you? . . . Your heavenly Father already knows all your needs, and he will give you all you need from day to day if you live for him.

Matthew 6:30, 32-33, NLT

God Knows What You Need

Dear Heavenly Father,

Help us not to get so entangled in our own needs and problems that we forget that you are the giver of all good gifts and that you promise to meet all our needs.

You have assured us that we don't have to live in fear and stress, but we simply need to trust you. You graciously invite us to bring our finances and all other worries and needs to you.

Will you touch my friend with confidence and faith—even in the midst of any worries—as she rests in your promise to provide exactly what she needs?

Try to live in peace with everyone,
and seek to live a clean and holy life,
for those who are not holy will not see
the Lord.

Hebrews 12:14, NLT

Living in Peace

Dear Lord,

We want to see you, to be near you, to experience your presence and blessings in our lives!

I ask that you help my friend and me to live lives that are morally pleasing to you. Help us never to get caught up in the speech or lifestyle patterns of a profane and godless culture. And help us to be peacemakers in our families, churches, and communities through compassion and prayer.

We worship, praise, and thank you today for your gift of peace.

I myself have gained much joy and comfort from your love.

Philemon 1:7, NLT

Thank You

Dear God,

I am so grateful for the wonderful friend you have brought into my life to help me on my journey as a follower of Jesus Christ. She has given me great counsel and comfort. I have been challenged and encouraged. Prayers have come before your throne on my behalf because of the love she has for me.

I am so happy that the Christian walk is not a solitary trek. I am awed by the reality that when I grow closer to you, I grow closer to others, my friends, and my family.

You alone are perfect, and only you are absolutely trustworthy. Thank you that you have enriched my life so much with a friend who is like an angel to me.

Never let loyalty and kindness get away from you! Wear them like a necklace; write them deep within your heart. Then you will find favor with both God and people, and you will gain a good reputation.

Proverbs 3:3-4, NLT

A Good Reputation

Heavenly Father,

When we are loyal and kind, we attain favor from the people in our lives, and most of all, from you. Guard my friend's reputation so that it brings glory to your name.

I confess that at times I have coveted the high regard of others, but I want it without the inconvenience of extending myself through loyalty and kindness. I know there are no shortcuts to a good reputation. I pray that I would show kindness and loyalty to my friend at all times.

Help both of us to be a blessing to others—not just for the reward of a good reputation—but because it demonstrates our love and obedience to you.

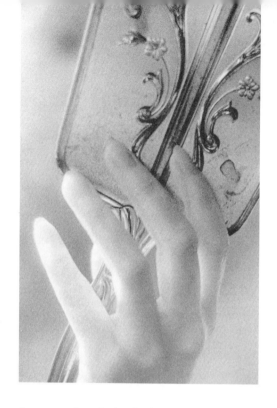

I am sure that God, who began the good work

within you, will continue his work until it is

finally finished on that day when Christ Jesus

comes back again.

Philippians 1:6, NLT

Not Finished Yet—
But Someday

Dear God,

My friend is growing in her faith. She is growing in her knowledge of your Word. She is growing in ministry and service to others. Like me, she sometimes falls short in her attitudes and actions, but I can see that she's still growing.

What a wonderful work you began in her life. You have given her peace, confidence, and gentleness.

On our final day on earth, dear God, whether it is because Jesus comes back to gather those who love him or because we face our moment of death, we look forward to seeing you face-to-face and knowing that your work in our lives has been perfected.

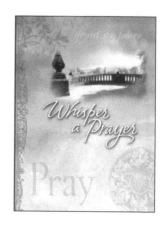

Also from Tyndale House Publishers

Whisper a Prayer (0-8423-8293-3)

Whisper a Prayer for Moms (0-8423-8295-X)

Available at your favorite local retailer.